HOW A FAMILY WAS MADE

by Paula Anderson

Illustrated by Nedra Lynch

HOW A FAMILY WAS MADE

Published in the United States of America

Grammy's Cottage Publishing
Shawnee, KS 66203

Book designed by Prairie Smoke Consulting
Belton, Missouri 64012

ISBN-10: 0990324907

ISBN-13: 978-0990324904

This book is dedicated to families everywhere.

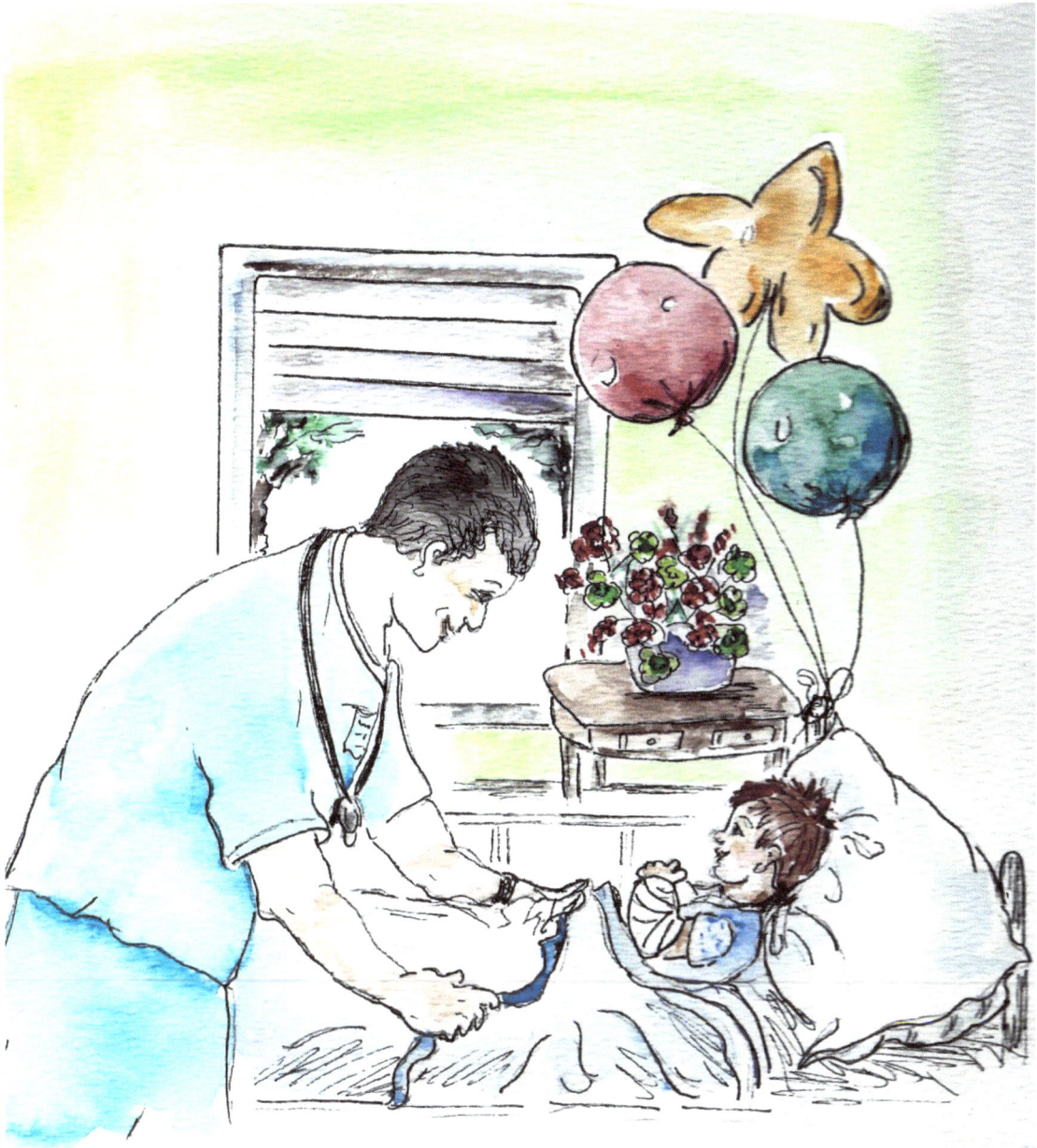

Daddy Evans is a nurse. He works hard taking care of sick people.

Mama Evans loves to cook and bake. Mama and Daddy
have a little girl. Her name is Lily.

Lily has long pretty blonde hair with hazel eyes and loves to play with her dog, Angel.

She dresses Angel up like a baby.

Lily is excited! Mama is almost ready to have a new baby and her tummy is big. Grammy stays with Lily while Mama and Daddy go to the hospital.

Grammy takes Lily to the hospital to see Mama and her new little sister, Roma. Lily loves the baby the minute she sees her. She looks like a little doll. She has soft brown hair and hazel eyes like Lily's.

Lily helps Mama take care of her baby sister.

Silly Grammy is so proud of the growing little family.
She takes lots of pictures of them.

They are a happy family of four.

Baby Roma grows up fast. She loves doing everything Lily does. Angel is always with them.

The girls are getting big. Mama and Daddy decide they want more children. It will be fun to have a baby in the house again!

They go to an adoption agency. It is a place where babies stay who don't have a Mama and Daddy to take care of them.

One of the ladies hands Mama a tiny baby wrapped in a blue blanket. Mama and Daddy sign papers promising to take good care of the baby.

Mama and Daddy take the baby out to their car. They put the tiny babe into a new car seat and drive home.

Mama goes inside and sits in her rocking chair. Lily and Roma are very excited. "Mama, let us see the baby!"

15

Mama unwraps the little baby, dressed in blue clothes. The baby is a BOY! His face is the color of hot chocolate. His eyes are big, black, and round. He looks at the two girls.

Lily touches his tiny head, covered with soft black curls like a baby lamb. "Mama, can I keep him?" asks Lily. Roma moves in close so she can touch him too.

"My baby!" says Roma, pouting.

Mama says, "Girls, girls! We *all* get to keep him. His name is Isaiah." Now they are a family of five!

Soon Isaiah is a toddler. The telephone rings. The nice lady at the adoption agency has exciting news for Mommy, Daddy, Lily, Roma, and Isaiah. "We get to bring home a new baby today!" says Mama.

18

A *second* baby brother arrives at the Evans' house!
His black hair is braided on top of his head and his face
is the color of dark chocolate pudding! "His name is
Benjamin and we will call him Ben," Daddy tells them.
They are a family of six!

Babies grow into toddlers and soon Ben is walking and running. The phone rings again!

The family brings home a *third* baby brother! His name is Nehemiah. He has lots of fluffy black hair and is the color of chocolate cake.

The Evans family goes to court and Judge Sloan says they may keep the three little boys.

Isaiah, Ben and Nehemiah have found their "forever" family!

The family enjoys living in their pretty gray house with red shutters and a big tree out front. The children love to run and play in the big back yard.

Now the *little* family is a *big* family of seven: Daddy, Mama, Lily, Roma, Isaiah, Ben and Nehemiah Evans.

THE END

In memory of sweet Angel

Paula Anderson
Photograph by Gene Ann Newcomer

This fun little story was written by a real Grammy! Paula Anderson has always loved to write. This is her first published work. Watch for more of her children's stories in the future.

Paula lives in Kansas with her husband and son, a dog named Sam, and three cats, and she really does have five grandchildren! In future books she will tell the story of Sam and maybe even more stories about her grandchildren.

For more about Paula and her writing adventures go to:
https://www.facebook.com/GrammysClutteredCottage

Nedra Lynch
Photograph by Paula Anderson

Nedra Lynch has been doodling, drawing and spattering paint since she could hold a crayon. She doesn't know when she started creating art; it has been something she does naturally. Nedra says, "As I paint mostly animals and country life, this adventure into children's illustration has been a joy."

Nedra shows and sells her work at Globe Art and Glass Studio and Gallery in Globe, Kansas; a tiny town west of Baldwin City, Kansas. To see more of her work, go to: www.globeartglass.com

www.ingramcontent.com/pod-product-compliance
Lightning Source LLC
LaVergne TN
LVHW072057070426
835508LV00002B/146